MW01596153

Dedication

I am blessed to have had a walking angel as my mother.

Thank you for always believing in me Mom, and may you rest in eternal peace.

(Marguerite "Sauti" Wills May 20th, 1949-February 19th, 2010)

To my Aunt Harriet and Ms. Andre Hill, (my second mother), both whom lost their battles with cervical cancer.

This book is dedicated to all survivors of ovarian and gynecological cancers, families, caregivers and those who lost the battle.

May you thrive and live every day to the fullest.

To those who lost the battle, may your voices be heard through your loved ones, as we advocate for more research, testing and a cure.

Copyright © 2017 Serena T. Wills

Published By:

Divine Wryte, LLC

Printed in the United States of America

ISBN 13: 9781974278022

ISBN 10: 1974278026

Library of Congress Registration Number: TXu 2-003-984

All rights reserved. No part of the book may be reproduced in any form without prior written permission from the publisher, except by a reviewer who may quote brief quotes and excerpts used in reviews.

Dearest Dr. Tornature,

5/2018

Crying Tears of Teal

a book of poetry

by

Serena T. Wills

Contributors

Editing
Dawn Adams
Dawn@thetrainingground.us

Cover Art
David Rodriguez
www.drgorilla.com

Author Photo
Dee Hill
www.deehillphotography.com

Cover Design
Stacy Luecker
www.essexgraphix.com

Typesetting
Athena Shack
www.waterspringsmedia.com

Artists

Riki Johnson-Atkins
prettyrikiart@gmail.com
Paintings

David Rodriguez
Paintings
www.drgorilla.com

Jenice Johnson-Williams
Photography
www.artislife.gallery.com

Dee Hill
Photography
www.deehillphotography.com

Samax Amen
Illustrator
www.samaxamen.com

Jedigoddess
Painting
www.jedigoddess.com

Table of Contents

Table of Contents

Acknowledgements

For the air, I breathe, ability to walk, move, smell, touch...the gift of life couldn't be possible without my Heavenly Father, God and my Lord and Savior Jesus Christ. Thank you, for blessing me and allowing the gift of words that you bestowed in me to touch others.

To all those we've lost, now in heaven, I say, "Ase" to you. Ase (pronounced AH-SHAY) in West Africa means to acknowledge the ancestors.

My lovely and beautiful mother, Marguerite "Sauti" Wills, you instilled so much in me. From you, I learned to embrace my talents, to be passionate, to be an advocate for what is right and a servant to the community and I wouldn't be who I am without you. I miss you so much and although God called you home on February 19, 2010, when your battle with ovarian cancer was over, your memories and legacy will live on through our family and me.

I aspire to be a great mother like you and I know you will guide me as I raise my beautiful son, Jordan. He is the light in my life and a blessing from heaven. Your selfless love caused you to adopt two medically challenged children after you had me. You're now with my sister Ayana. Christina has turned into "Nana's little helper." You'd be so proud of her, as Nana said, "She's an extension of Mom." That she is. God also blessed me with another sister in 2000 when I learned about my father's side of the family.

Shavonn Hayes, you are truly a wonder and I know that you grew to love my mother as I love yours. Keep moving forward Sis and achieve great things. I have a lot of sisters from other mothers that I grew up with and I love each of you.

Venetta Renee Pittman, you have been by my side since 1987 when we met in middle school. Thank you for your love, guidance, support and till this day we have never had an argument. We have misunderstandings, talk about it and move along. You have been with me through the thick and thin. Bless you!

My Nana, Mrs. Bernice Wills, you are the rock and elder of our family. Your strength is truly divine. You've endured so much loss but continue to smile at the future and what you have gained. The love you bestow on your family is priceless and you have truly handled the loss of Mom with the grace of God. I can only wish that I will grow old and be as strong as you one day.

My beautiful son Jordan...there aren't enough words to describe the happiness that you bring me. When your grandmother passed away, I thought I would never smile again or know how to love someone new so soon. Then you came into my life in 2011 and my God, I have smiled, loved and laughed immensely. Your eyes melt my soul and your laugh makes me giggle. Thank you, beautiful child, for choosing me as your mother. I will make sure to tell you all the great things about your grandmother and other ancestors.

Uncles and Aunts are a blessing and if you have them, like I do, then love up on them. Aunt Hilda, Kirk, Uncle Larry and Annette; all of you came together to pray, watch over and care for Mom while she was sick with ovarian cancer. I know the plan was for all of you to grow old together, God had something else in store. Mom left with each of you a love like no other. She will watch over each of you and your children from heaven and whenever you miss her, just look up and feel her smiling at you through the rays of sunshine.

Extended Aunts Kim Black and Yvette McBean, I don't know what we would have done without the two of you. You were two of Mom's closest friends. Your visits, calls and smiles meant the world to her and the family. I truly believe that family is more than just blood. It's the love that the two of you showed to us and Mom through the last six months of her life. I know you have lost a sister physically, but you gained a heavenly one that will be with you day and night.

I have a plethora of cousins, but one visited Mom every month, made her laugh, bought her candy when she wasn't supposed to eat any and was by my side the day she closed her eyes and went home to be with the Lord. Fern Fisher, we now have to advocate for gynecological cancers as we lost Aunt Harriet as well in 1997. I needed you that night and you were there; such a beautiful spirit and I know you will continue to shine through all your days.

God blesses us with soldiers, who are there through the thick and thin. I learned a valuable lesson from 2009-2010. Some friends will step up and be in the front line with you and some...will fade to the back. True colors are shown at a time of sickness and death. When the storm clouds are gone, you know who your true friends are and who you can lean on (even when the times are good). But they have shown their true colors and they look good to me!

So many to thank who went through the most difficult journey of my life. You know who you are between cooking food, rides back and forth to NYC, checking in on me, having a key to my house and being there when I came home, praying for us, driving hours for one night, flying in, sitting with Mom reading her passages from the Bible. God is truly awesome and has blessed me with incredible friends that I call my family. God bless all of the children and young adults in my life that are my godchildren and nephews. Thanks for checking on me and making me smile during this difficult time. Children truly light the world.

Thank you to the artist of the cover David Rodriguez of Dallas, TX, Stacy Lueker of Essex Graphix for the cover design, Athena Shack for the typesetting of the book and all her creative marketing skills and advice, the divine Dee Hill for my beautiful author photograph and my editor, Dawn Adams of the Training Ground, fans, artists who love me and pushed me forward, all of the places that let me vend my poetic products, books, hit the mic and embrace my artistry. I also want to thank the artists that contributed their art work to this book in various sections. David Rodriguez, Riki Johnson-Atkins, Jenice Johnson-Williams, Dee Hill, Jedigoddess and Samax Amen. Your work is amazing and I know it will touch everyone who reads this book!

Many blessings to my Ebenezer AME family that prayed for us. I am blessed with a dynamic duo that leads our beautiful church Pastor Grainger Browning Jr and Co Pastor Jo Ann Browning, the ministerial staff and members for being there for us. Lastly, I must thank special organizations that were there, not just for me but, for cancer patients, their families and friends as they deliver resources such as support groups, counseling, seminars and workshops on various cancers, patient support, etc.

Leukemia and Lymphoma Society (Team in Training) endurance program. Team in Training (TNT) raises millions of dollars for patients and their families that are suffering from blood cancers. I began training with this dynamic group in summer 2007 in North Texas and when I moved back to the DC area I ran my fifth marathon through the National Capital area chapter. Between the emails, cards and love from coaches, I was able to come back two weeks after Mom passed away, run 18 miles and later on complete my fifth full marathon in March of 2010. I couldn't have done it without you team. GO TEAM!

Life with Cancer is a nonprofit organization, housed in Northern Virginia. The physical center is in Fairfax, Virginia and they also offer services in Loudon County as well. All their groups, counseling workshops and events, take place outside of the hospital except for those receiving bedside attention at INOVA Hospital. Everything is free of charge. Between individual counseling, cancer caregiver, the GYN cancer and the Good Grief groups, they made the healing process so much better and taught me and my family, not only how to take care of my mother but ourselves as well. I wish there was a facility of this nature in every city across the country. Blessings will come to this organization, as you always have the doors open to those in need. Also, the DC Metro Chapter of the National Ovarian Cancer Coalition and Tia's Way which is dedicated to cervical cancer.

Introduction

I began writing this book throughout my mother's illness and shared some of the poems with her before her death from complications of ovarian cancer. It's a silent, fast moving and deadly cancer that is rarely talked about in our communities. On February 19, 2010, my Mom, Marguerite Wills, and I talked for hours on end before she passed away. I promised her, that I would educate women, teach the importance of getting annual checkups and be an advocate for ovarian and all gynecological cancers.

After meeting the ladies of the GYN cancer group at Life with Cancer Center, I decided to add more to this compilation of poetry and write a book dedicated to the survivors, those we've lost and the families that cared for them. This book serves both as a personal dedication to my mother; and to everyone who has suffered from ovarian and other GYN cancers. You will see uplifting poems such as "Storms and Awakening" that talk about people who were once sick but are now healed. Pieces such as, "Pain and Three Mothers" will tug on your heart strings as a person goes through the grief process and can't understand why their loved one is gone. The final journey in this book has uplifting pieces such as, "Living Life 155% and Regaining Momentum which are dedicated to the survivors.

You will smile, cry and laugh as you journey through these pages. The book includes blank pages for journaling your own thoughts and various statistics on ovarian and gynecological cancers. It's time to Break the Silence! Let's fight to end all cancer one dollar at a time, one step at a time and build a pathway towards freedom.

God bless you and may peace be with you. Mom...this one's for you!

Serena Wills

"Gynecologic cancers are cancers that
affect female reproductive organs, including
the ovaries, endometrium, uterus, cervix,
fallopian tubes, peritoneum, vagina and vulva.
Roughly 71,500 women in the United States
each year are diagnosed with a gynecologic
cancer, and the risk increases with age."

~ CANCER TREATMENT CENTERS OF AMERICA

Journey One

My steps have been ordered
Wish I could turn back the hands of time
The moment...I felt disorder in my body
No one could tell me it was cancer
And, that it was, the final answer
I've chosen to take those next steps
For my family and my personal health
Scared to death, what this road will lead to
Either way, I've chosen to fight and go full speed ahead
Taking...those...next...steps

Next Steps
By Jenice Johnson-Williams

Deeper Than Menopause

Praying it wasn't a deeper cause
To my diminishing health

Hoping it was just menopause
I don't even know how to begin
To tell my eldest—my best friend
The truth, that I have not been well
Untended ills, for years on end
Have caused these bizarre symptoms to exasperate
I'm on bended knees, praying it's not too late
To deal with whatever is going on
My days turn into nights and my nights turn into days

Then suddenly weeks have gone...Past...
And yet, I still can't bring myself to tell her
That I think the cause
Of my pain, bloating, constipation, heavy legs,

Shortness of breath and loss of appetite
Is deeper than menopause
Deeper than aging
Deeper than arthritis
God, I've got to call my daughter
And tell her...
I'm not well...
 Come with me to the hospital
I need an answer
Lord have mercy, please

Don't let this
Be something
Irreversible
Hoping whatever it is...
That it's curable

Cancer

Was my doctor's final answer

Lying in the cold hospital room

I thought it was pneumonia or anything with a cure

"Cancer," he said again

Hand to my chest...

"Wait doctor, wait...what does this mean?

I have a family to feed. I can't stay here indefinitely."

With heavy eyes, he studied the paper and began,

"This cancer has consumed your body,

Your CA-125 count was over 3000 and that's extremely high,

I cannot lie

It's a miracle you could walk into the hospital,

Large tumors have overtaken your stomach

Fluid is expunging from your ovaries, lungs and even your feet

You've advanced to stage four...don't be afraid to weep."

Head was spinning with terms that corroborated my final
diagnosis

"I'm sorry but I'm not through...

Your cancer is inoperable and there's not a lot we can do

You have two options that I will share

You can leave today, and do nothing at all

Or you can choose to fight with one of the cancer fighting
protocols

We'd insert a small port to administer the chemo,

With cancer fighting drugs like Neupogen or Tomixifen,

There are no guarantees, but some results have been
promising.

Whichever your choice, I must make sure you understand

I'm unable to say how long you will have

If you choose to fight, we'll do all that we can"

"I choose to fight but I'm going home. Please tell me what lies ahead?"

"Fatigue, nausea and naturally pain,

Hair and weight loss, appetite might be gone

and another side effect we call chemo brain.

Tell everyone you know there's a long road ahead."

I pulled the covers closer to comfort me

Pleading to God to carry me through this journey

Tired from all my symptoms

Exhausted from the knowledge of the cancer within

Clutching my discharge papers close to my side,

Praying that the prognosis will be on my side

I held on to the terms of my diagnosis

Stage four...

Ovarian cancer...

Life with Cancer

Do I scream or cry
Sob or try
To comprehend this illness that is
Haunting my body
Should I shout
Be angry
Or just give up the fight
Before even starting
I don't know how to live with cancer
Normalcy is a thing of the past
Asking doctors question after question
Afraid to know my fate...
Am I going to live?
Stage 4 is what they told me
Staring through tears at the doctor's report
Speechless
My kids...my husband...my dear mama
What will they do without me?
Wait a minute...wait a minute!
God! Why am I writing myself off?
I know what the papers say
But what do You have for me?
Do I go on and fight?
Chemo or a clinical trial?

Or just go home?

Naturopath or herbal treatments

Let me know which way to go

Life with cancer isn't easy

Watching people walk by,

No cares in the world

I want to live!

I want to be healed!

But I don't know which way to go...

I'm not alone...

I have people in my corner

A few couldn't handle my news

They left me high and dry

But they will be the same ones crying over my coffin when I die

God help me to live my life and get back to normalcy...to my sweet and loving family

Praying steadily that the pain will go away

That the tumors will shrink and vanish

Tremors will be no more

Vision will be clear again

Yes...yes!

I'm going to fight!

I'm not ready to go into the light

My body may be weak...

But my spirit is strong

Let's start this fight

I'm ready for the battle against cancer

But this battle is not mine... it's Yours

So, let's do this together God

Envisioning my body...totally healed

Sitting in a recliner in the hospital

My first round of chemo...

Listening to my mama's constant encouragement

Delighting in my children's hugs

Savoring the kiss my husband plants on my forehead

God, I'm ready for battle

It might be uphill

But I will

Win the fight!

Next Steps

Wrapping myself in a crocheted blanket

Back and forth in grandma's rickety rocking chair

Sipping on hot ginger tea

Meditating on my plan B

Replaying my doctor's words in my head

"It's cancer...stage 4... deny treatment and

There's nothing else to be said"

Felt like my dreams were smashed to pieces

Plan A was no more

I cried out...I bellowed...

JESUS!

JESUS!

Why me?

JESUS!

Please let me be!

Healthy again

Kept rockin' in Grandma's old den

Meditating on my next steps

Although angry with my diagnosis

I'm very blessed

Gifted with a dad and siblings who love me

A dream job I adore and

A fiancée, despite my illness said, "Marry me."

Slowly getting up to walk

Step by step I began to talk

Out loud

Channeling my grandma and ma who I lost to this devil already

With every step, more tears poured out of me

Slowly talking to myself,

"Beat this devil disease,

may my life be filled with ease,

after this storm,

let all the blessings of heaven,

swarm around me,

break the vicious cycle

cancer no more...

cancer no more...

cancer no more!"

Picking up my pace a bit

Pain from my belly to the tips of my toes

All I want to do is just sit

But I've decided, "I won't quit!"

Finally, reaching my destination

Leaning on the warped telephone table

Dialing the 10 digits

An uplifting voice, "Welcome to the Oncology Department...how can I assist you?"

Slowly, I uttered the words,

"I'm not ready to quit...I need to schedule my first treatment,

But it will be done in God's way,

I want to be healed, both integrative and medically

I refuse to be in a casket and lie next to grandma and ma.

My name is Bella Armstrong

And I'm ready for my next steps

So, I can become a walking testimony for others to see

That some cancers can be temporary

Please send someone to come and get me.

My steps are ordered and I'm finally ready.

I'm finally ready...

Finally, ready to fight so this cancer will be no more."

*Bella Armstrong is a fictitious name used for this poem

Journal Notes

Journal Notes

_____

_____

_____

_____

_____

_____

_____

_____

_____

_____

_____

_____

_____

_____

Journal Notes

_____

_____

_____

_____

_____

_____

_____

_____

_____

_____

_____

_____

_____

"Cervical Cancer: tends to occur during
midlife. Most cases are found in women under
the age of 50, and it is linked to human
papillomaviruses (HPV)."

~   CANCER TREATMENT CENTERS OF AMERICA

Journey Two

Crying Tears of Teal

Tears sparkling like reflections of the sun off a lake
Day by day I visit you and make
Wishes and ask God for your body to heal
I want your spirit to shine as bright as the color teal
Praying you can come home with me one day
Yet I cry tears of teal
Hoping that God hears
And sees the streaks on my face are tears of hope
Envisioning a future with my mother
As I cope
With her diagnosis
I won't give up...
I wish my tears...
Could wash away her pain

Battlefield Part 1

Sitting

Waiting

Patiently

As I watch the drip...drip...drip

Of an IV bag that's supposed to help me

Alone in my hospital room...I made it my place of restoration

A medical team of doctors invading my peace

I don't want to hear one more negative thing

Surrounding, they ask how I am doing

"Hmmph, I could be better these days,

Got needles stuck in my arms,

a port about to be imbedded into my body

and you ask ...how am I doing?"

I didn't mean to snap

But it's bad enough I can barely take a nap

My mind overtaken by thoughts of never leaving this place

At times the morphine hits and I feel like I'm in outer space

But when I finally drift into a shadow of deep sleep

There's always someone tapping me awake

"Time for your medicine or almost time to eat."

The lead doctor stands over me with his clipboard in hand

"I want you to know that you're making *some* progress

But we're worried this cancer doesn't seem like it wants to rest

We'd like to try a different type of chemo, of all the options...it's the best."

I've heard all this before and I don't feel like hearing it any
more

"Let's talk about something natural, a somewhat different approach,

all these drugs in my system, they can only do so much

It feels like they're killin' me, not curing me...ya feel me?

So explain to me Doc...what else do you have for me?"

Battlefield Part 2

They huddled for a few

Hushed phrases volleying back and forth

Opening door halts discussions as my daughter steps forth

The weight of the silence, stirs her intuition and speaks through her subdued smile

She knew something wasn't agreeing with my spirit

The lead doctor welcomes her and bids her to sit with me

He drones on and on and on

I pray for swift healing to walk outta here and leave this misery behind

My daughter's head shakes his words away

"Doc...we're at war and the enemy is cancer. I'm done with this illness touring my mother's body. Let's agree on a battle plan to defeat this wicked disease!"

Smiling with pride, at my daughter's determination to go, fight and win

Thinking to myself so I may begin...

A renewed life...at home

My beautiful home on the beach

Waiting to welcome me once again

Mother and daughter joined in solidarity

I want to fight in a healthier way

I refuse to be pumped up and bowed down to more chemo

Tired of wasting away...

Losing hair...

Losing memories...

SERENA T. WILLS

"So Doc, what's it gonna be?"

Excusing his posse, he faced us alone

He spoke with assurance underlying his tone

"I think you can teach me a thing or two.

No matter what, I'll see you through

Let's revise the plan of action

So, we can conquer this thing

We'll battle it together, side by side, until the victorious end."

Finally, I thought we're getting somewhere

Thankful I spoke up

Praying that a new treatment will give me a fighting chance

To win this battle called cancer.

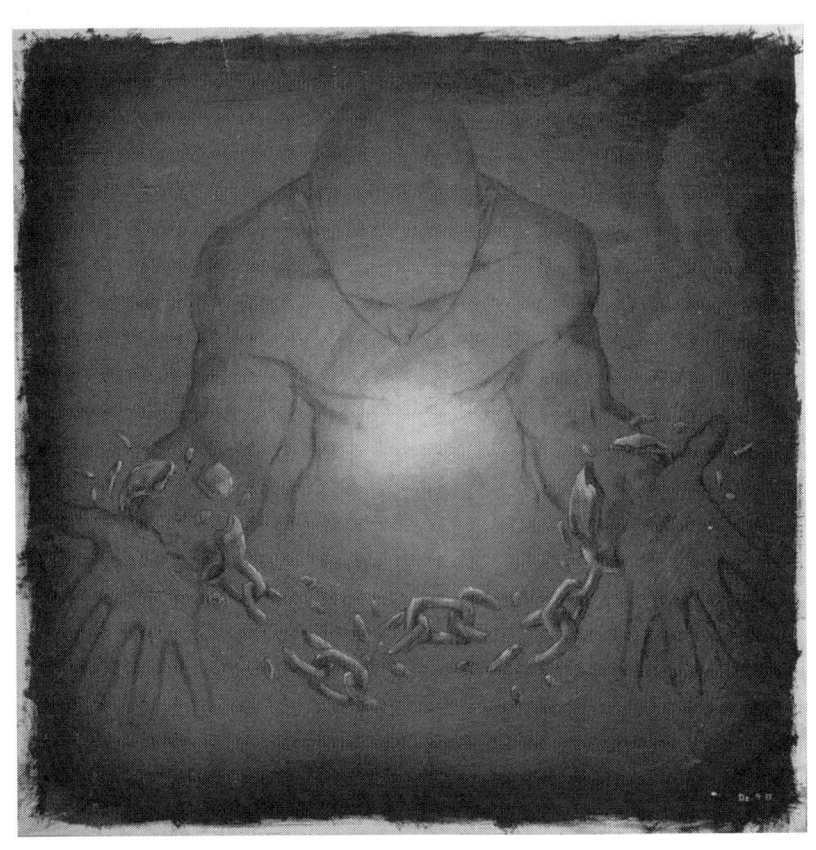

Broken
By David Rodriguez

Crying Tears of Teal

Tears glistening against my skin

A sea of water streaming down my face

Uncontrollable, I felt hopeless

God, I've got to save her...I love her and I don't want to let go

How can she be stricken with cancer...my mother...the woman I adore!

Locking myself in a room so I won't upset her

Crying tears of teal for ovarian cancer

I went from a daughter to a caregiver

"Mommy please don't give up the fight

We can win this battle together...right?"

Crying together, I began to see a wave of teal

Promising each other to go on day by day

Hoping to God that there is a way for her to stay

I cry tears of teal, like I suffered a battle wound

Back and forth like a yo-yo

Trying to find answers to a diagnosis that I can't swallow

Wallowing in my pain...tired of these tear stains

Crying to God my tears of teal

I wish this whole episode in our life wasn't real

Hoping He answers and you will soon heal

So, we can stop crying tears of teal

All Around Me
By David Rodriguez

Muddled Thoughts

Darkness swept around me

Thoughts of losing another love or someone else dying

Ransacked my brain cells

Shaking my head in disbelief

This can't be happening to me again

The new millennium

We've been through so much

It's a wonder that I'm still standing

Watched the towers go down,

Pentagon in flames

Flight in fields in Pennsylvania

Lost due to an overtaking

Prayed that as the years crept by

The anguish would extinguish

Yet, it keeps snowballing

Things seem to be running into each other

I can't keep up with all the sad news

Muddled in my thoughts

One bad thing after another

News of friends fading away

Being called home at such a young age

It's mind boggling to me

I shouldn't question God,

Do I have the right?

● SERENA T. WILLS

I'm hesitant to ask why...have so many died before their time

I want to know why one love after another seems to not work

Will I be alone forever or is he really out there for me

These thoughts race through my head continuously

Enough to make me go crazy

Ending the first decade of the new millennium

With my mother's diagnosis

The one person I have left to depend on

Seems to be fading

Quickly before my very eyes

Cancer they said...fast moving at that

God, I ask, have I done anything

Are you preparing me for something greater?

Darkness so thick it will choke me, if I let it

Fighting against it, praying for it to turn into light

Muddled thoughts brewing,

Constantly whipping my brain, my heart and spirit

Crying in the middle of the night

Make my muddled thoughts disappear

God please make them fade

Muddled thoughts, they seem everlasting and all I can do is pray...

Sweet Dreams

My days are too long
Hours go by too slow
Living my life in a diseased body is brutal
Between the pain, constant spasms, disequilibrium,

brain fog, neuro problems, joint aches, anxiety,

depression, dizzy spells and 24/7 nausea
Doctors talking, lab work, needles and IVs
It's a part of my daily routine
Wanting to end my days from the moment I arise

As evening comes I get excited
But sadness hovers as I long for nightfall
It's the only time of day I have some peace of mind
I close my eyes and have sweet dreams
The days when I graced the stage
Through dance
Free to use my gifts to move others emotionally

Times of normalcy
Now unattainable in the daytime hours, it's a mere fantasy
Dreams of walking down tree-lined streets
Something that used to come so naturally
One dream I sat in a coffee shop overlooking the ocean
Not one care in the world
Loving life once again completely
I dream of flying kites and parasailing, flying to distant lands

Building castles with my sweet son on beaches of white sand
I felt the sand sift through my finger
Felt the breeze off the ocean on my scalp
My dreams seem so real
Amazing is the power that I feel

Yet when I wake up
I'm isolated once again
Body plagued with symptoms

SERENA T. WILLS

Praying to God for the day He will heal them

I sometimes lie awake
Wanting my eyes to close again
So I can have another
Sweet dream

Whimsical Moments

You are my air
Into your eyes I stare
Knowing that I received the ultimate prize
You as a mother
And I as your daughter
Still moments in time

Will be remembered forever
Watching you grace the stage with dance
Deep conversations about forgiveness and giving others a
second chance
The night you held me tight when I heard my father died
Wiping away a steady flow of tears as I cried
Being my warrior through many battles
Dry days to stark nights you were my water
Pouring energy into my valley like a flowing river
I don't know what I will do
When God calls you home
I know I'll have memories that float through my brain as
whimsical moments
In my heart you'll always be
Whimsical
Like cherry blossom petals that travel on a spring breeze
And Blooming Marguerite flowers in France
Praying to God that as the seconds, minutes and days go on

These moments will come more with ease
But for now let's share the time we have
Creating memories that will be kept
Whimsical moments we'll always have
Beyond your last breath

Journal Notes

_____

_____

_____

_____

_____

_____

_____

_____

_____

_____

_____

_____

_____

_____

Journal Notes

_____

_____

_____

_____

_____

_____

_____

_____

_____

_____

_____

_____

_____

_____

Journal Notes

_____

_____

_____

_____

_____

_____

_____

_____

_____

_____

_____

_____

_____

_____

Journey Three

Loss

Brain on overdrive
Mama is no longer alive
Blaming myself
Replaying over and over
What more I could have done
The Father of the Holy Son has spoken
Continuously looking
For answers,
As to why she had to die
Alas I can't find them
So then had to ask myself
How would she have been
If she had stayed
Sick, filled with cancerous thoughts
Should I have let go,
I told her it was okay to go
Or did I make a mistake by telling her so
The biggest loss of my life
Left to pick up the pieces of my broken puzzle
Incomplete,
One of the pieces is gone forever

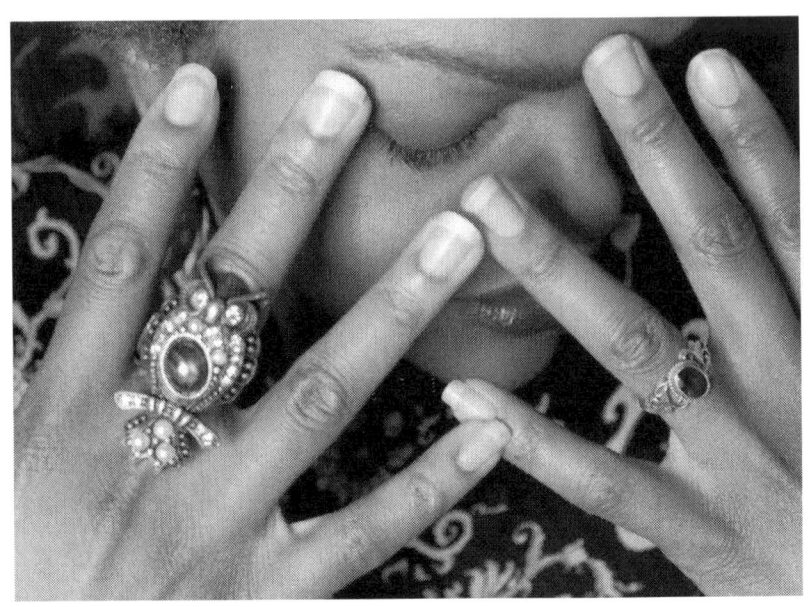

Photo Taken By Dee Hill,
person photographed,
Jenice Johnson-Williams

Pain

Healing relieves me of pain
But makes room for more
Empty space begins to fill with easier breaths,

less crying and hopes of nothing else
Happening to me
When the pain of a loved one's death,

A broken relationship, or hate-filled job

Have subsided...
The devil gives you more
Nights are occupied again with misty eyes,

Palpitating heart and no rest
Still managing the loss of my sister
Two and a half years later now my mother is gone
Like a wound that never healed quite right
Reopened, now it hurts even more than before
I never thought I'd be a motherless child
So soon...
Down a sister, father, papa and now my mother
Like the story of Paul, the pain piercing my side

I thought it was the devil
God, I don't know how much more I can take
Please forgive me if I've done anything

To you to allow me to go through this
I'm reliving everything I've done wrong

I need to know why I'm being punished
I'm not a bad person
I don't understand why you took my Iya so soon
Pastor told me the thorn you feel is keeping you humble,

The greater the pain, the bigger your anointing

God will bless you
Shaking my head, wiping the constant stream of tears

● SERENA T. WILLS

Why me God...why us
Family going nuts because now she has left us
Praying for more healing, as the minutes, hours, days and weeks go by
Dreaming about her at night, hoping when I wake up it's all a lie
Hoping she will call and say, "Baby I'm home."
But alas, "This number is now disconnected" confirms that she is really gone

God give me faith to believe, in the end, this will all make sense
For now I have to come to grips
With Mommy's death
Healing relieves pain
Sometimes it makes room for more
Standing on my faith
Asking God for strength and
Everlasting guidance since

He's given me a guardian angel
Leaning into your spiritual arms Mommy
Missing you
Praying that my healing comes and pain will be subdued
Hoping in time, it will be easier to manage
The pain of losing you...

The Flood

Memories flood my brain
Every crevice is touched as they pour down like rain
Some good and some not
Times when I see smiles and blowing out birthday candles
Suddenly obscured by doctors lingo, nurses chatter and Mom's
ailing body
How I wish the past
Would gently push out the way of the last
Moments as such
Sorrow is pain
Needed in order to grieve
Praying that I receive
Healing memories that are buried deep within
Out of those 172 days from diagnosis to the end
I can amend some thoughts
Times which were enduring
Most of Mom's illness
Important convos, walking down memory lane
Days when she kept me sane
Holding hands, wiping tears from her face

Whispering it's going to be okay
Did I lie to her?
Hoping they'd find a cure
To save my mom, her spirit was so pure
Asking for her forgiveness
Flashbacks of the bad times invade
Precious space that I need to save

Golden spiritual mementos that need placement
Instead, I'm sometimes stricken with nightmares
Wondering if I will stay in this sick state

Die in the middle of the night

Or awaken to healing

I'm still searching

Searching

Searching
For an everlasting cleansing of this intensifying illness

Praying for a flood of divine thoughts

Flood waters through my body to heal

Restore the whole me

If not physical, then God give me eternal cleansing

Anything to be me again

The Flood
By Jedigoddess

Three Mothers

Human instincts want to know

Why three mothers are gone

In four short months

So young and ready to see their children

Get married, have children and love on their families

Sickness swarmed into their lives

Like bees flying through the sky

Not comprehending why

Our mothers

Are gone

No wedding bells or being walked down the aisle

No motherly advice to help colicky children sleep at night

Moments as we pick up the phone

Realizing seconds later you aren't there...you're gone

All of us are mourning our mamas

Who were here one day and gone the next

Sickness overtook these beautiful women

Wishing we could have reached inside

And cured them as Jesus did in the good book

We aren't Him

If we were, there would be healing all over this world

Life would be perfect

If we could save...

Surrendering confusion, blaming fingers that we point at

ourselves

Because we couldn't rectify the problem

Cancer, emphysema and diabetes were all the causes

There will be many more...

Make us strong enough to help others who will mourn their losses

In the meantime, we grieve over three mothers

Died in four months

Simple problems and complaints

No longer can be tolerated

Ears go deaf to those who aren't grateful

Arguing with their parents

Ignoring that they are borrowed...

On loan to us from God

Children...get it right

Siblings...stop the fights

We don't know what's next

Love each other until the end

Because there are six children now

Grieving, crying and screaming for their three mothers

Praying for healing

One day the open scar of death, grief, pain and sickness

Will be gone

Memories will last on

God let us be examples

To those children

Who don't appreciate their mothers

For we lost three

In a matter of two seasons

Three

In a matter of four months

Three mothers gone to be with the Father

Our God and the heavens

That will eventually ease our pain

Until then...we grieve

Our three mothers and the many others

We say to you

Ase...Ase...Ase

Help us from the ancestral realm

Continue to love us from above

Always and beyond

Silent Tears

Streaking my face
Creating a puddle of water in my lap
Deep breaths as I let out shrieks of pain
Grief untamed
Falling to my knees
Screaming please
Please...
Come back to me
Alas in the stillness of the night
Begging and pleading
Reasoning with God

I tried to tell Him
"We had plans, my man, and now my mother has been taken
from me."
Shoulders hunched over
Arms wrapped around my stomach
Releasing the sorrow and aches trapped within

Mourning over Mommy
Thought she would make it
Instead God turned the clock forward
Minutes passed by and moments are unclear
Surreal that she's gone

Phone silent
No more ringing in the middle of the night
Ever since Mommy walked into the light
Thinking back to the day
When she smiled at me to say
"I love you and you'll be okay"

Not comprehending
Riddles she made
But as I pieced it all together I finally realize
She was preparing me

Always a mother even after the last breath
Worried about her family
Reassured her we'll keep each other lifted

As God covers us like a blanket on a cold winter day
Fast forward to now
Visions of your smile
Dancing in heavens clouds
Brings joy to my saddened heart
Comforted by your spiritual presence

That surrounds me day in and day out
Even the times when I shout
"Mommy where are you!"
I'm reminded...

As I feel a gentle touch rub my back
And a whisper...I'm right here baby girl
Mommy you will always be with me
And I will be with you too
My sorrow is raw
Emotions crashing like waves against a mountain wall
Rescue me from this grief
Send me a sign
That you're thinking of me too
Figuring out my next steps

And what God has ordered for me to do
The only thing missing is you
Gazing into the dark night
Blurred vision from tears
Praying to God to heal my family and me too
Sending a message to you
Through prayers and thoughts
I love you
Honored that God chose me to be birthed through you
One courageous, bold, vocal and loving woman
Your legacy will be kept alive

I will keep the promises I made to you

Loving you...always...

Silent tears fall as I grieve

Ancestor's Call

Shaken by my dream

My daughter visited me once again

Confused as to what to do

Spirit is conflicted

Contemplating on my final passage

She touched my hand as she spoke, "Mom I've missed you so. Please join me and receive a reprieve from your suffering."

Her offer sounded good, but what about my loved ones I'd leave behind

Father wrapped his arms around me, with a hug he gave me permission to be whole again

Caught in between two worlds

Heavenly places vs. earthly pain

Placing my face in my hands I sobbed

"Daddy I'm so sick and tired, cancer has whipped me physically, but how do I leave our family?"

He sat and the glow from his being was delighting and healing

Rubbing my back gently he smiled, "It's not easy. I don't want to see you suffering any longer. Join us and be with the Father and Son, who've carried you through this final journey."

Watching them walk away, I had a lot to think about

As they got down the path my father waved and whispered

"Join me..."

Standing was something I hadn't done

In the many months that had come and gone

I walked towards the light where I heard the trumpets blow

My pace was slow but as I neared the gates my loved ones passed through

I reached out and then snatched my hand back

Wiping away tears I cried, "I hear the call but I have one last message to give to all. Let me go back and say goodbye to my family before I die."

Awoken from my dream by the poke and prod of a needle

Groggy, I told the nurse, "I saw them."

She replied, "I believe you darling, but it was all a dream."

She walked away, then stood frozen in the doorway

Her Caribbean accent rang as she asked, "What more can I do for you?"

"My kidneys are failing, cancer is all over my body, vision is blurry, skin is itchy...please call my family."

She obeyed my request with a simple nod

Slowly turning my head towards the window, I saw the sunset

In the distance and I heard my ancestors call

The trumpets blew and I knew my time was coming to an end

God brought me peace, I wasn't scared anymore

Morning arose and my family surrounded me once more

Thankful for that last conversation, it sent sensations that tickled my toes

I got my last wish, my family is bonded, united and love is in season for them again

Closing my eyes that evening, I told my heavenly family I'm ready

Felt the hands of my father, daughter, grandmothers and all

Thank you, God for letting me say goodbye and giving me peace

As the storms of cancer

Are no more

Responding to my ancestor's call

Wisdom
By David Rodriguez

Journal Notes

_____

_____

_____

_____

_____

_____

_____

_____

_____

_____

_____

_____

_____

_____

Journal Notes

_____

_____

_____

_____

_____

_____

_____

_____

_____

_____

_____

_____

_____

_____

_____

Journal Notes

_____

_____

_____

_____

_____

_____

_____

_____

_____

_____

_____

_____

_____

_____

"Endometrial Cancer: is rare for women under the age of 45; most cases are found in women over 50. However, it is the most common gynecologic cancer as well as uterine cancer which affect more than 52,000 women annually in the US."

~   CANCER TREATMENT CENTERS OF AMERICA

Journey Four

Divine Rebirth...
Death Begins New Life

Standing on my own two feet
Body is perfectly molded
My hair has grown
Emanating a radiant glow
Light shines all around me
I wish my family could see
I'm living life again
I'm divinely reborn
Long steps to meet my maker
Bowing down, I trembled
Placing His hand upon me
Commending me on a job well done
One final request I made
Can I watch over my family from the hilltop?
As their new life begins
Wish was granted
I walked on discovering my new self
Death of me has brought on new life
Comforting my daughters crying at night,
Heavenly breaths from above, I sweep away their tears
Divine rebirth for me, will be one for them
Helping them heal, whispering in their ears...
"Please don't weep or fear...I'm healed
My life is eternal
Divinely reborn"

Into the Light
By Riki Johnson-Atkins

Divine Rebirth

Earth Stood Still
Heavens Gates Opened
Cancer finally cured
Scared at first of
What lie ahead
I remember fighting for breath in my body
Saying good bye
Closed eyes once lead to visions of drugs, chemo, hateful
needles and pain
Ability to walk was nonexistent
But this time
Oh this time
When I closed my eyes
I woke up to streets of gold, hugging my Daddy and my little
girl as they greeted me
Feeling my full face, color restored, and my tight dancer calves
have returned
I'm whole
Free
Smiled as I felt my beautiful natural hair that's all grown in
Daddy and Ayana led me to a shining light
Bright as it gleamed into what was once a dark sky
Huge arms extended
Embracing me, rubbing my head

The Lord hugged me, "Sauti...job well done.
You carried enough crosses in your life, now it's time for you
to rest."
Staring into the eyes of the Great One I asked, "What about
my loved ones, those left behind? How will they do?"
He raised his arms and clouds above displayed the perfect view
I saw my loved ones as they grieved over me
Tears of those who cared for me
I reached out and they felt my touch

My mother, daughters and siblings startled

God said, "They felt your touch, talk to them. Tell them their grief will be brief and their mourning will be replaced with healing."

Whispering...I'm here and near...don't cry no more over me.

The tears of my mother were suddenly replaced with her smile
Family now laughing about the good times
God said, "Rest, for there is some work to do...time to move road blocks, barriers, and clear storms.
Rearrange their lives so they can live comfortably
Bless the doctors and nurses that cared for you
All those you touched for it's their turn to be blessed in return." I smiled and when I went to walk away the huge arm extended to me again
"I ask you to do one last favor for me. Go down the road into the house on the hilltop and be happy with what you see."
Guardian angels led me to the house and there I saw old relatives and friends
African drums started beating, awakening my spirit as I danced like I was back with my dance company
Celebrating my rebirth of eternal life
All day I praised Him and then in the corner I saw a baby cooing and playing

I knelt down to play with him and saw me in him
Confused I asked Ayana, "Who's child is this?"
She smiled and said, "Meet your grandson, you must spend time with him and prepare him for that magical journey."
I picked up my grand and was led into a majestic room in the back accented with silver and gold.

A huge bed and a view of the valley
Papa tapped me on the shoulder and said, "Marguerite, put your feet up, rest up and welcome home."
It felt good to lay down after 20+ years, no worries, I will take care of my family from afar, playing with my cooing grandson
Feet kicked up, being fed and nurtured by ancestors
I'm at peace, no more suffering, yelling ouch when you roll

me, no more memory lapses due to chemotherapy
Don't mourn...I live on a hilltop, my special place picked out
by God
Resting...finally...eternally

Restful Spirit
By David Rodriguez

SERENA T. WILLS

Faded Tears

Smiles faded

The pain still fresh

Losing Mama

Tear streaked faces

As the procession, marched on

Paying their final respects

Bells chiming

Songs awaiting

As the choir sang Amazing Grace

Closed eyes

Tears streaming

As time moved on

She spoke to her Mama

Leaned over the casket

And whispered, "thank you."

Laying a hand on her Mama's soft cheek

She leaned over and whispered again, "Mama I love you."

As she spoke

Family gathered around

Whispered... "Thank You."

Seats are filled, standing room only

The pastor stood at the pulpit

She stood frozen and leaned over for that final kiss

"Mama may your spirit live on and through me."

Whimpers getting louder as the Pastor gave the benediction

Tears streaming

As her smile began to return

The sorrow, still so fresh, began to fade away

Mama is at peace now

No more pain

No more suffering

No more tests or chemo

Her spirit runs free through the grassy meadows the Lord grew just for her

A garden of violets awaits her

She now looks over her family

One breath, two breaths...

Tears are unstoppable

As she lifts her arms up to the heavens and thanks God for her Mama

Family and friends join her

For what is now a celebration of her life

The procession leads to the cemetery

As the final prayer is spoken, she begins to weep

Spirit feeling lighter

The tears wash away the pain

She goes home and plays her Mama's favorite church song

The smile that faded years ago returns

She realizes her Mama's death should be mourned

But her life should also be celebrated

So that her soul and spirit live on

She revels in the sweet memories of her Mama

She will not weep because she now knows she is not gone.

Warm Breeze

As the warm breeze hit my face

I knew that, "It was done."

All my problems and burdens

Were conquered

God told me years ago

"Wait on me child and I will see everything through."

Nights I cried, wondering how bills would be paid

Days went by wondering why my sister's health was fading away

God kept telling me, "I'm coming to your rescue; I'll walk with you and take you through."

Watching the sun leave the sky

As the moon peered through my blinds

Still wondering how I'll make it through

Suddenly I felt a presence

In my space

Not understanding what or where it stood

My Grandma once told me, "Chile there are times when God is in your space and you will know it when you feel Him."

God began to work through me

Around me

All for me

Burdens were lifted

Unanswered problems resolved

Bills were paid in full

I now understand that God comes in His time

He heard my sister asking for Him

Take me with you God

For I am done

Her health failed

And she went to Him

Her battle was over

And her job here on earth was done

God said, "Let it be done, let her be whole and may this life be complete."

I listened to Him

As He conquered not just my worry

Fears

Anxiety

He also gave me peace, comfort, love and a feeling of serenity

Reborn
By David Rodriguez

White Candles

White candles burn

Sweet aroma

Vanilla

Gardenia

Jasmine

White rose

Cleansing

Restoring a calm that was lost

Glowing flame gives my spirit light

Ancestors are lifted

Flickering in the still of the night

Crackling wick is all I hear in the dark

White candles give me peace

Lift my hope like a dove flying through the sky

On my knees praying

Placing white flowers beside the pictures of the smiling faces of those lost

Remembering them through the gift of the light of my burning candles

I reminisce on lessons learned

Mother said to never yearn for the dead

She taught me to light beautiful white candles

To talk to those who've gone on

They will be your listening ear, she said

She promised, *"When I'm gone I'll always be near to hear and guide you.*"

I believe her

Her light is shining through me

Symbolizing purity and peace

Something I thought I would never feel again

Simple things have helped me grieve

Although she had to leave

I talk to her

Every day and every night

Promising her that one day, I'll feel joy again

Calmness is building inside me

And one day...I'll even feel as bright as the color white

My passion will be on fire, like the wick that burns

I promise...one day...I'll feel like those white candles

Sound of Your Voice

The sound of your voice
Calmed me in the midst of a storm
Soothed me during a cry when I just couldn't take it anymore
Loving sense of always knowing when I needed an, "I love you
and that's all I called for."
Encouraged me when I needed to get up...stand up after
taking a hard fall
You always knew what to say
How to say it
When to say it
Timing was always perfect
Sixth sense would kick in
Didn't understand how you always knew
Ears that could hear miles away

Caught in a lie because I didn't want to worry you
You would say, "You're not alright...talk to me."
Whether filled with rage from being done wrong or simply
missing you from so far away
Somehow...some way...you always knew when I had to hear
your voice
I long for our daily calls, filled with laughter, tears and even
the occasional silence between us
Pouring out tears for you because I can't have those days any
more
Voice sang to my spirit every single day
I miss those days

Yet, I'm so blessed to have had them
Today, I heard wind chimes clang as the breeze blew through
my window
I know it was you stopping by
To say, "I came by to say I love you."
I couldn't see you, but I felt you
And heard your gentle whispers as I lifted my hands high to
praise Him for the love we shared

Blowing kisses to heaven saying, "Mama...I love you too."
The sound of your sweet voice was music to my spirit and soul

Runway to Heaven

Heaven and earth sing

Our ancestors ring

The bells

Each chime to alert of someone new approaching the gates

As I day dreamed

I looked up to the clouds

Settling over the city lights

Heard the thunder clap loudly

From a distance

As dusk fell

With colors of purple and pink galore

Forming straight lines through the sky

Like a runway to heaven

A cloud formed a huge hand

I would like to think it was

God's hands coming down

For the first time my eyes witnessed

No separation of my world and heaven

Began envisioning the runway to this paradise

A place where people no longer suffer

The land of milk and honey

Where the grass is always green

The birds are always singing

And people love unconditionally

Whether I feel a breeze in my home

Smell the scent of my daddy's fragranced oil

Or my mother's smile upon my son's face

A leaf of my peace lily perking up

Sometimes when the page of my scriptures turn on its own

I know my Grandma Verma is close by

Each time, I'm reminded that they are always near

As they descend on earth from time to time to see what's happening

Protecting us constantly

Guiding us to a better life as they assist God our Father with healing, and loving us

I envision the runway to heaven full of light

Bells chiming

And those huge hands I saw in the clouds

Leading them to paradise

Heaven isn't far

If you believe

Runway to Heaven
By Jenice Johnson-Williams

Journal Notes

_____

_____

_____

_____

_____

_____

_____

_____

_____

_____

_____

_____

_____

_____

_____

Journal Notes

_____

_____

_____

_____

_____

_____

_____

_____

_____

_____

_____

_____

_____

_____

Journal Notes

_____

_____

_____

_____

_____

_____

_____

_____

_____

_____

_____

_____

_____

"Ovarian Cancer: affects up to 5% of women who have it in their family histories. It has the highest mortality of the gynecologic cancers, killing more than 14,000 women annually in the United States."

~ CANCER TREATMENT CENTER OF AMERICA

Journey Five

Storms...
"Sometimes They End Up Good"

Days and nights once collided
Chemo brain haunted my sweet memories
Needles that had injections with my name on it are now in the
past
Instead of cancer still being here I'm now standing up at long
last
Cancer is no more as it went away day by day
I'm free from being shackled to my bed
Brain cells slowly returning to a new normal instead
I can embrace my family without it hurting me
Storms are sometimes filled with blessings, if you believe
If you were me, then you would see
Just how good the storm turned out to be
Now I must heal, yet continue the quest to get answers
While I fight for my friends still in the midst of the storm
called cancer
Time to rebuild my body so I can live on
Storm clouds cleared and the sun now sits in the sky alone
That sun I couldn't see while battling my
storm...called...cancer

Storms

Silence

Listening to the sounds of the rain outside my window

Drip, splash, drip, splash

Splashing on the leaves as the water pours out of the sky

Voice of God becoming stronger while the wind picks up

Tree branches scratching my windows

On bending knees praying for the healing rejuvenation and restoration for Mama

Struck with cancer two months ago

Hurricane like winds

Whipping devastation to her physical being

Bleakness blinds my vision

Grim nightmares brewed with thoughts of Mama possibly leaving me here on earth alone

Lights flickered

Storm becoming fierce

Similar to the one Mama is enduring

Memories of walking hand in hand with her a year ago

Ignorant to the fact that we're not invincible

Although God's children

We're human susceptible to diseases, anguish, hurt and pain

Throat closing as streaks of tears are accompanied by screams

Confessing with my mouth all the things I did

Not comprehending

Mama's diagnosis

She's my rock, the living angel in my life

Overnight I became Mama's wall holding her up

Who knew I'd be strong enough to bear so much on my spirit, soul and mind

Blurred eyes, wet pillow and sore throat...

Believing faithfully that as the cancer dies Mama's body is being reconstructed

Optimism growing from the pain,

Believing God kissed the cancer goodbye

Matter of time before she's healed

Body stretched across the floor

Praying for a total breakthrough

Rain falling

Slowly decreasing

Water tumbling off the leaves

Cancer cells dying

Disease stricken storm

Dying...leaving the body

Renewed

Healed

Cured

Storms
By Jenice Johnson-Williams

Regaining Momentum

Borderline of life and death

Shining light on my face

Arms extended to me

Loved ones who don't want to see me in pain

Wanting my body to heal

I hear my daughter who passed three years ago

Telling me, "Mommy I miss you."

I walk towards her into the light

Then it hit me

My work isn't done here

Hands haven't touched all that God has for me

Mind working overtime

Which way do I go

Do I walk towards my beloved child that I miss

Or make an about face to the family that still needs me

My grandchild yet to be born, who needs his grandma

Eldest daughter screaming, "Mama don't go; please wake up"

Sitting straight up

Legs moving

Toes wiggling

Chest pains no more

Pinching myself

God told me at the end of the dream

It's not your time to move on with us

SERENA T. WILLS

Your daughter and loved ones are willing to wait for you on this side

Go back to the others and heal

Touch more lives

Love more children

And be a mother like never before

For the first time in months

I stood to my feet

Walked over to the curtains

And tore them open

Sun shining on me

Smiling face

Nurses amazed

Doctor looked as if he was going to faint

I'm healed

Ready to make a difference

Like never before

Time to regain momentum

Catch up on lost time

Visit those who've prayed over me

Get that child of mine married off so she can have my grandbaby

I'M ALIVE

Awake and steady

Baby steps to the bathroom

Something so natural, I haven't done in months

Sitting down feeling relieved

Got up and packed my bags

Turned to the doctors and told them, "I gotta go."

Checked myself out and hailed down a cab

Home is calling me

Not my heavenly one as they told me..."Not yet"

But my home where my mama awaits me

Daughters who love me through and through

Brother and sister who prayed for miracles

I'm alive and well

Regaining strength

Momentum

Keeping the faith

That I won't be alone

As thousands will be like me

Healed and cancer free

Regaining my life

Forming a relationship with God like never before

I...AM...BACK

Loving life faithfully

Living every day like it's my last

I...AM...HEALED AND CURED

Liberation
By Riki Johnson-Atkins

Survivor

I SURVIVED!

CANCER IS NO LONGER ALIVE

IN MY BLOOD, ORGANS AND WHOLE BODY!

Now I'm not going to lie

All the while I was sick with this wretched illness I knew I would survive

Yeah I was scared

At times, I dreamt of my death bed

But when I awoke I knew I was given another day

One more chance to get better as I lay

In a hospital bed

I was even told hospice might be my only bet

I didn't believe those lies and instead I fought on and survived!

I SURVIVED!

Chemo treatments, blood transfusions, surgeries, organs removed

Half my weight gone and hair is a total loss

Kept telling myself, "This is temporary, I dare not go insane

all that I've lost, I will regain."

So I fought!

Even when the doctors thought I was going to die

One day at a time, I was revived!

Rehab was my friend

    I was once strapped to my bed in diapers and such

SERENA T. WILLS

Step by step I learned to walk again

Finally able to walk to the bathroom

A place I hadn't seen in months

Inch by inch I fed myself more

Sun was shining the day when my doctor laid

His hand on top of mine and said, "Your cancer is gone."

Tears poured out of my eyes as I declared, "Hmmmmph I told you I would survive!"

5 years later, I'm still free

I have what you call maintenance

And still must do some physical therapy

I believed...I prayed...I told myself affirmations and surrounded myself with those who had faith

I told everyone then and I will tell you the same

MARK MY WORDS EVERYONE

I...WILL...SURVIVE!

"Dedicated to the survivors, keep thriving and surviving!"

Survivor
By Jenice Johnson-Williams

Living Life 155%

I run
Walk
Skydive
Parasail
Bike Ride
Mountain Climb
Advocate for my friends with cancer
Who are fighting to stay alive
I'm a...
Mother, Lover
Wife, Sister
Writer, Leader
And you ask how do I do it all????
I live and take chances and risks
For those who are too cautious, I say, "tsk, tsk, tsk."
I live life 155%
100% isn't good enough for me
Once I became free
I promised to live life naturally
Living every moment as if it's my last
Traveling from city to city
But still you ask
"How do I find the energy?"
It's very simple...you see...
Just 2 years ago I was given 6 months to live
I thought I'd given everything that I could give
But it wasn't enough...
The doctors were about to give up
I vowed if I made it
To live my life wholly
Made my dream checklist
I gave myself a "D" day
My "D" stands for Destiny!!!
"D" stands for Discharge!
"D" stands for Determination!

Determined" to restart my life over, it was a must
Got rid of the non-believers, doubters and pure haters
Encircled myself with those who stood the test of time in my
darkest moments
Fighting to get my life back I went after my "destiny"
Each day I check off something from my long checklist
And every day I add more to it
I'm living life like my girl, Jill Scott, it's Golden
Living Life 155%
If for some reason you dare resent how I live
Then see yourself to the door
And if anything your stupid doubts gave me more
Fuel to my fire
As I live out my life's desire
Until God calls me home

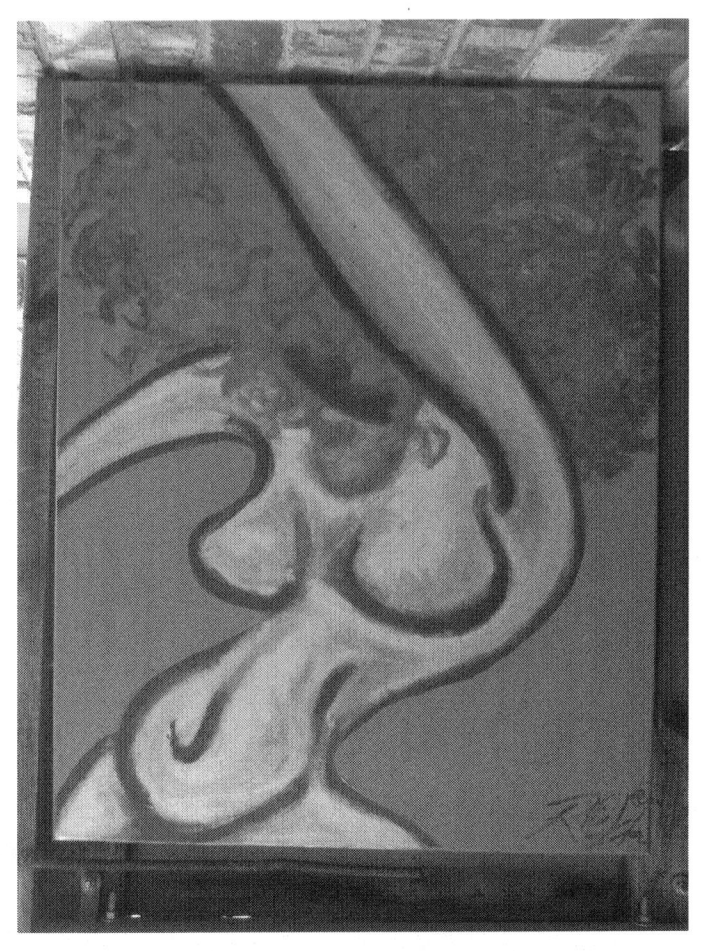

Joy
By Riki Johnson-Atkins

Teal Mementos

Color as bright as a peacock's feathers

A mermaid's tail

Flower petals whisked away in the wind

Almost the color of clear blue water

Gentle waves dance around your feet

Clear stones made bright blue reflecting the sunlight

Teal Topaz gemstones that encircle a neckline

Bold blue representing a new you

Decorating a room in hues of emerald green and teal blue

Wind chimes that move to the soft breeze

As the earth inhales and exhales through my window pane

Breathing in the new beginning of a total restart

Placing a ribbon on your chest

As you join the rest

Of your sisters that battled Ovarian cancer

A sea of teal before the Capitol steps

Shouting for a cure, more research and tests

So no one else has to stress over this wicked killer

Teal mementos adorn the households of thousands

The bold yet beautiful

Gentle to the eyes and soft to the touch

Teal hearts that will soon heal the masses

Lives that were once colored midnight blue

Now have a new hue

SERENA T. WILLS

With some zeal

Called Teal

With a splash of wonderful mementos reminding you of your days ahead

And all that you've gone through

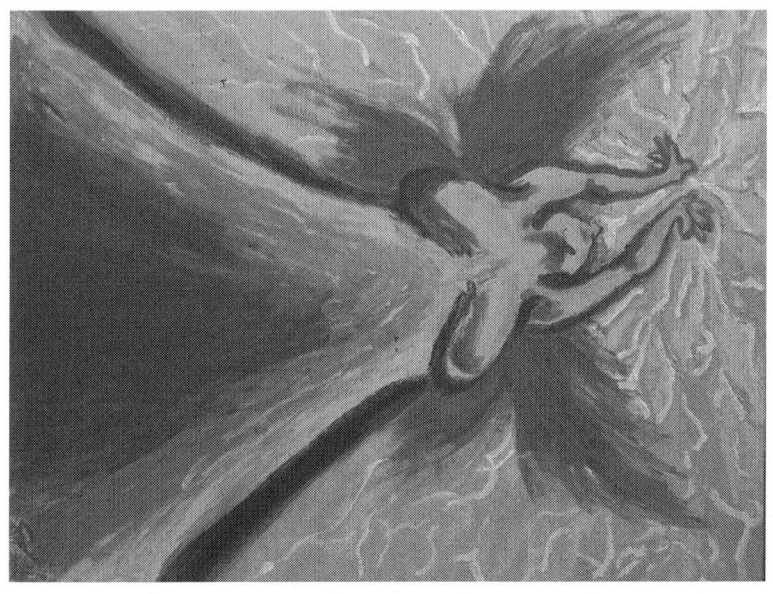

Salvation
By Riki Johnson-Atkins

Journal Notes

_____

_____

_____

_____

_____

_____

_____

_____

_____

_____

_____

_____

_____

_____

Journal Notes

_____

_____

_____

_____

_____

_____

_____

_____

_____

_____

_____

_____

_____

_____

Journal Notes

"The key to lowering the risk for these
cancers is preventive care and early diagnosis.
And for many women that may mean taking
time out from busy family and work schedules
to put their health first."

~   CANCER TREATMENT CENTERS OF AMERICA

Outro

This book was a compilation of the various emotions experienced and expressed while at my mother's side during her six-month battle with ovarian cancer and from sharing the journey of the survivors and their loved ones, I got to know through the Life with Cancer Center in Fairfax, Virginia, and the National Ovarian Cancer Coalition. These warriors/survivors, look forward to better days ahead even when they had/have dark days and most amazing thing is that despite all, they live every moment to the fullest.

I decided to take a stand for ovarian and all gynecological cancers through my poetry and became an advocate because of my mother. I wanted to write a book that showed my compassion towards those who suffer(ed) from cancer, in particular gynecological cancers. I continue the fight and pray that one day there is a cure for all.

If you want to learn more about how you can help us with the fight, please go to www.cancer.org If your fight is more specific such as ovarian, please go to www.ovarian.org for the National Ovarian Cancer Coalition or **www.ocrfa.org** for the Ovarian Cancer Research Fund Alliance.

Thank you for supporting this book and becoming an advocate for more research to be done and a cure to be discovered!

About the Author

Serena Theresa Wills is a native New Yorker and currently resides in the Washington, DC area. She holds a Bachelor of Arts Degree in Policy Studies from Syracuse University and a Master Degree in Public Administration from Virginia Tech. She is currently pursuing a Master of Arts in Health and Wellness Coaching with a concentration in integrative health practices and nutrition at the Maryland University of Integrative Health (MUIH).

During her literary journey, Serena moved to Dallas, Texas for three and half years, where she focused on honing her craft and became published. She completed several manuscripts and children's stories, while there.

Her first published book, *"Reconstruction, Pieces of Life Volume 1, A Book of Poetry"* was released summer 2014. This book of poetry takes a journey through the various emotional

SERENA T. WILLS

stages of a person who believed their happiness could be found in another person until they experienced heartbreak. After a transformation, they discover where their true happiness and purpose lives.

Her authoring credits include contributions in the following publications: Gumbo for the Soul, Here's Our Child Where's the Village and Gumbo for the Soul, "Women of Honor–Special Pink Edition edited by Beverly Black-Johnson, Have a Little Faith, Keeping the Faith and Love. Hope. Faith. edited by Vanessa Miller and How I Freed My Soul, Liberated Muse, Volume 1 and Betrayal Wears a Pretty Face, Liberated Muse, Volume 2 and Creases Expelled from the Fold, edited by Khadijah Ali-Coleman and Cornbread, Fish and Collard Greens: Prayers, Poems and Affirmations for People Living with HIV/AIDS, edited by Khafre Abif. She is also a health and wellness writer for various blogs and online magazines.

Serena has worked in the nonprofit field for twenty years, concentrating on youth development, literacy and health and arts education.

Serena is a mother, and health advocate and spends her spare time enjoying family, traveling, running, African dance and serving her community through the sisterhood of Delta Sigma Theta Sorority, Inc.

For more information on her publications, events, listening bar of poetry, blog and more, visit her website at **www.serenawills.com**

One Phenomenal Woman...Life with Marguerite "Sauti" Wills

Marguerite Teresa Wills was born May 20th, 1949 in Jamaica, NY. Born to the late, Mr. Lawrence Wills, Sr and survived by her mother Mrs. Bernice Wills. They were more than tickled to receive such a blessing from God. She was a loving sister, and as the eldest of five, she took her role seriously. Tales of their childhood on the block, to this day, will make anyone laugh. From stories of her being chased by her father when she came home late, to the dog chasing her sister down the driveway and her brother and his friends tearing up the garage and Nana's grass playing basketball, to the stories of her late sisters, Doretha and Evalena, splashing water into the mean neighbor's yard, there was never a dull moment in the Wills' household.

Throughout her childhood, Marguerite stayed active through dance. She practiced ballet, tap and jazz at Bernice Johnson Dance School (BJ's). She graduated from St. Michael High School in Brooklyn, NY in 1967. Then a shift happened. She said between the African drums that called her down the

SERENA T. WILLS

hall at BJ's after she took ballet and the liberation movement taking root in the nation, she began to transform. Although quiet and reserved, she spoke the knowledge of elders and advocated for what was right. She cut out her perm and changed her name to "Sauti" which means "voice" in Swahili. Working at Green Lantern, she helped with free lunch programs and organizations such as the Black Panther's to help teach our children about equality and to fight for the Civil Rights.

She joined the "International Afrikan American Ballet" (IAAB) and performed in the first of many shows, which is now the world renowned "Dance Africa." In the 1970s, both she and the nonprofit dance troupe performed or what we refer to as, "Tore up the stage" all over the state and in Canada. This was her life and IAAB went on until the 80s to dance together as one. Now 40 years later, Dance Africa is known all over the world.

Although she held jobs at CBS Records and JCPenney, she always said she wasn't cut out to work 9-5pm as she wanted to put more time, effort and dedication into IAAB. One day as she danced, she began to feel a bit tired and discovered she was pregnant. She danced until it was time to give birth to Serena Theresa Wills in 1975. She became a homemaker to tend to her daughter and still continued to be active in IAAB.

Her life then took on another shift as God called her to work with children in need. Dorethea Washington was diagnosed with AIDS in 1983, but delivered a beautiful daughter named Ayana. She held on until she knew that her daughter would be taken care of. Marguerite stepped up to the plate and said, "I'll take her home." The doctors said Ayana wouldn't see the age of 1. Because of Marguerite's constant love, attention to all her medical conditions such as severe brain damage, scoliosis, and under developed organs, Ayana lived until the age of 24 before passing away in 2007.

Marguerite instilled her beliefs into her daughter Serena.

As a volunteer through her high school at Terrance Cardinal Cooke in Harlem, Serena met Christina. Born in 1989 to a crack addicted mother, Christina was brought to the facility where they thought she would die or be severely brain damaged because of the drugs in her mother's system. After a few visits Marguerite couldn't bear to leave Christina in the facility and adopted her in 1993. Christina is now 27 years old and is known as "Nana's Little Helper." Diagnosed as Autistic with very little communication, she helps with grocery shopping, cleaning, laundry, and even puts Nana to bed at night.

She was an advocate for children that had special needs and always envisioned opening a group home for more children. She tried to start a program, but, alas, the state made major cuts. She continued to care for her children and stayed fighting for their rights. Anyone could tell you that Marguerite's African name "Sauti" was appropriately given to her, as she never backed down and in the end she always won.

The last turn of her path was when Marguerite was diagnosed on August 10th, 2009 with Stage IV Ovarian cancer that had spread to her stomach. Her determination to live went on for months. Not understanding why at first, she understood at the end and now she smiles down on us. Her last task on earth was to reunite her family and make it known that tomorrow isn't promised to anyone. She cracked jokes, was always friendly with the nurses and doctors and never complained. Her journey ended on Friday, February 19th, 2010.

There isn't enough room on the page to describe her. She traveled many paths that led to her touching the lives of many people.

Resources

Information is Power (Resources and Organizations that Support Cancer Patients, Families and Research)

American Cancer Society
www.cancer.org

Cancer Treatment Centers of America
www.cancercenter.com

Georgetown University Hospital (Lombardi Comprehensive Cancer Center)
http://lombardi.georgetown.edu/

Jamaica Hospital Palliative Care
http://jamaicahospital.org/pages/clinical-services/palliative-care-cs

INOVA Health System
www.inova.org

Leukemia and Lymphoma Society
www.lls.org

Life with Cancer
www.lifewithcancer.org

National Institute of Health

www.nih.gov

National Ovarian Cancer Coalition

www.ovarian.org

Ovarian Cancer Research Fund Alliance

www.ovariancancer.org

Susan G. Komen

http://ww5.komen.org/

Team in Training

www.teamintraining.org

The Sidney Kimmel Comprehensive Cancer Center at John's Hopkins

www.hopkinsmedicine.org/kimmel_cancer_center

Reconstruction, Pieces of Life, Volume 1

A book of Poetry
By Serena Wills

Epiphany... Musical Lovemaking

Lovemaking to my soul

Reaching down into places

Where no one should go

But somehow you're there with the power

Of your voice singing blues and your guitar

Strumming the chords of my creative muse

Musical depth of the oceans floor

Longing for a moment with you

Visualization of musically twisted thoughts

Poetry with your grooves

Rhythm and blues

Reggae to even country tunes

Tapping into me...

Dear Love...

Dear Love

I thought I knew you

Once adored your every move

Your style and grace

How is it that the thing I love

Could be so hurtful

The kind of love I thought I had

Was something that I envisioned to be untouchable

Approachable and something like no other

Again I failed at love, at what I thought it was supposed to be

Wondering if one day I will find that one

That will love me for who I am, my spirit and everything

He will look past my flaws and love me for my inner beauty...

Great Journey

Passion flows through my veins

Like the water falls in Zimbabwe

My love is as strong as the crashing waves of the Indian Ocean

Romance is as mellow as the sun setting over the Egyptian Pyramids

Heart as big as the continent of Africa

I AM ME!

Knowledge to pass onto others that seek Sankofa

Nurturing my loved ones as a Mother who loves her child

Thoughts of my future...please me

Those in my life are the pillars in my temple

Holding me up through the good and dismal

One who holds my hand, feels the strength of a warrior

And the knowledge of an elder

Those who embrace me feel the warmth of the sun as it blazes over the Sahara Desert

I AM ME!...

PREVIEW

Awakening Pieces of Life Volume 2

A book of Poetry
By Serena Wills

Healed Wounds

Scars that were deep
Bleeding profusely nonstop
Battle wounds from loving the wrong people
Losing my friends and family tragically
Broken love from a man I once adored
Questioning whether I'm being punished
If I did something wrong to deserve this
Crawling to the rock where I see people standing strong
I reached out and then it dawned on me
My wounds each told a story
Test became my testimony
The more I extended my arm I began to see
The wounds healing...

Da Flip!

This is how I feel
Your life has been flipped upside down
360 degrees
You didn't ask for it, you didn't want it
The confusion that has commenced over night
But it's here and there is no need to fuss and fight
It's here and you didn't want it
Your life got flipped upside down
360 degrees

Because she wasn't careful

She wasn't careful

See baby girl was confused

And as her mama sang the blues

And Daddy went to prison

She was in a state of confusion and needed intervention...

You Don't Know My Pain

You don't know my pain

Chronically ill for months

Feeling like I'm about to go insane

You don't know my pain

Crying out to God in the middle of the night

Asking Him to spare my life once again

Multiple issues clashing together

People not understanding brushing everything off

Family in denial because I'm always the health nut

Yet I feel so alone and in a rut

You don't know my pain

Suffering and in a financial strain

Waking up daily for months feeling drained...

SERENE
By Samax Amen

Contact

For more information on events, book signings, how to book the artist and creative products, please go to www.serenawills.com or email serenawills@yahoo.com

Also, please join Serena Wills on Facebook at www.facebook.com/serenawills and on Twitter @divinewryte.

 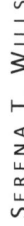

81771400R00068

Made in the USA
Lexington, KY
21 February 2018